Acclaim for J. Philippe Rushton's
Race, Evolutio...

"(An) incendiary thesis....that separate ... evolved different reproductive strategies to cope with ...erent environments and that these strategies led to physical differences in brain size and hence in intelligence. Human beings who evolved in the warm but highly unpredictable environment of Africa adopted a strategy of high reproduction, while human beings who migrated to the hostile cold of Europe and northern Asia took to producing fewer children but nurturing them more carefully."

---Malcolm W. Browne, *New York Times Book Review*

"Rushton is a serious scholar who has assembled serious data. Consider just one example: brain size. The empirical reality, verified by numerous modern studies, including several based on magnetic resonance imaging, is that a significant and substantial relationship does exist between brain size and measured intelligence after body size is taken into account and that the races do have different distributions of brain size."

---Charles Murray, Afterword to *The Bell Curve*

"Describes hundreds of studies worldwide that show a consistent pattern of human racial differences in such characteristics as intelligence, brain size, genital size, strength of sex drive, reproductive potency, industriousness, sociability, and rule following. On each of these variables, the groups are aligned in the order: Orientals, Caucasians, Blacks."

---Mark Snyderman, *National Review*

"Rushton's *Race, Evolution, and Behavior*...is an attempt to understand [race] differences in terms of life-history evolution....Perhaps there ultimately will be some serious contribution from the traditional smoke-and-mirrors social science treatment of IQ, but for now Rushton's framework is essentially the only game in town."

---Henry Harpending, *Evolutionary Anthropology*

Race, Evolution, and Behavior:

A Life History Perspective

2nd Special Abridged Edition

J. Philippe Rushton

Race, Evolution, and Behavior
2nd Special Abridged Edition
Copyright @ 2000 by J. Philippe Rushton
All rights reserved.

Published by the Charles Darwin Research Institute
Port Huron, MI

1st (1995) and 2nd (1997) Unabridged editions published
by Transaction Publishers, New Brunswick, NJ.

Japanese translation of 1st edition published by
Hakuhin-sha of Tokyo (1996).

1st Special Abridged Edition published
by Transaction Publishers (1999).

Library of Congress Card Number: 00-103721
ISBN: 0-9656836-2-1
Printed in the United States of America

Rushton, J. Philippe, 1943-
Race, Evolution, and Behavior: A Life History
Perspective/J. Philippe Rushton. — 2nd spec. ab. ed.
[GN 281:4.R87   2000]

Author

J. Philippe Rushton is a professor of psychology at the University of Western Ontario, London, Ontario, Canada. Rushton holds two doctorates from the University of London (Ph.D. and D.Sc) and is a Fellow of the John Simon Guggenheim Foundation, the American Association for the Advancement of Science, and the American, British, and Canadian Psychological Associations. He is also a member of the Behavior Genetics Association, the Human Behavior and Evolution Society, and the Society for Neuroscience. Rushton has published six books and nearly 200 articles. In 1992 the Institute for Scientific Information ranked him the 22nd most published psychologist and the 11th most cited. Professor Rushton is listed in *Who's Who in Science and Technology, Who's Who in International Authors, and Who's Who in Canada.*

Contents

Preface to 2nd
Special Abridged Edition

The first printing of this Special Abridged Edition appeared in 1999 by Transaction Publishers. It followed up on their successful 1995 and 1997 publications of the 1st and 2nd unabridged editions and a Japanese translation published by Hakuhin-sha in 1996.

However, when Transaction distributed thousands of copies of the Special Abridged Edition in a mass mailing to academics, a firestorm of controversy engulfed them. Although the Abridged Edition presented the same research in a condensed and popularly written style, similar to that used for articles in *Discover Magazine, Reader's Digest,* and *Scientific American,* the Progressive Sociologists, and some other self-styled "anti-racists," threatened Transaction with loss of a booth at annual meetings, advertising space in journals, and access to mailing lists if they continued to send it out.

Transaction caved in to this pressure, withdrew from publishing the book, and even apologized. Transaction's letter of apology appeared on the inside front cover of their flagship journal *Society* (January/February, 2000). Accounts of the affair appeared in *The Chronicle of Higher Education* (January 14, 2000), Canada's *National Post* (January 31, 2000), the *National Report* (February 28, 2000), and elsewhere.

Why the attempt to trash or suppress this booklet? Because there is no stronger taboo today than talking about race. In many cases, just being accused of "racism" can get you fired. Yet, teachers in America know the races differ in school achievement; policemen know the races differ in crime rates; social workers know the races differ in rates of welfare dependency or getting infected with AIDS. And sports fans know that Blacks excel at boxing, basketball, and running. They all wonder why. Some blame poverty, White racism, and the legacy of slavery. Although many doubt that "White racism" really tells the whole story, few dare share their doubts. When it comes to race, do you really dare to say what you think?

Racial groups differ much more widely than many people realize. Yet vocal groups in academia and the media simply forbid letting the public in on an open discussion. Many worry that just mentioning that the races differ creates stereotypes and limits opportunities. But looking at race does not mean ignoring individuals. It may even help us become more aware of each person's special needs.

This book presents the scientific evidence that race is a biological reality that has both scientific and everyday meaning. Other recent books on the issue are: *The Bell Curve* (the 1994 best seller by Richard Herrnstein and Charles Murray), *Why Race Matters* (a 1997 book by philosopher Michael Levin), *The g Factor* (a 1998 book by psychologist Arthur Jensen), and *TABOO: Why Black Athletes Dominate Sports and Why We Are Afraid to Talk About It* (a recent book by award winning journalist Jon Entine).

For more detailed information on any of the topics in this Special Abridged Edition, please read the corresponding sections in one of the unabridged editions, which contain over 1,000 references to the scholarly literature, a glossary, complete name and subject indexes, and 65 tables and figures. You can also point and click to the www.charlesdarwinresearch.org which published this booklet for more information.

May, 2000   J. Philippe Rushton
                                          Department of Psychology
                                       University of Western Ontario,
                                    London, Ontario, Canada N6A 5C2

1

Race Is More Than Skin Deep

Is race real? Do the races differ in behavior as well as in body? Are such views just the result of white racism? Modern science shows a three-way pattern of race differences in both physical traits and behavior. On average, Orientals are slower to mature, less fertile, less sexually active, less aggressive, and have larger brains and higher IQ scores. Blacks are at the other pole. Whites fall in the middle, but closer to Orientals than to Blacks.

White men can't jump. Asian men can't either. But according to Jon Entine's new book, *Taboo: Why Black Athletes Dominate Sports and Why We Are Afraid to Talk About It,* Black men — and women — sure can. The usual reason given for Black athletic success is that Blacks have little chance to get ahead elsewhere. But Entine's new book shows that in sports, Blacks have a genetic edge.

The physical facts Entine reviews are quite well known. Compared to Whites, Blacks have narrower hips which gives them a more efficient stride. They have a shorter sitting height which provides a higher center of gravity and a better balance. They have wider shoulders, less body fat, and more muscle. Their muscles include more fast twitch muscles which produce power. Blacks have from 3 to 19% more of the sex hormone testosterone than Whites or East Asians. The testosterone translates into more explosive energy.

Entine points out that these physical advantages give Blacks the edge in sports like boxing, basketball, football, and sprinting. However, some of these race differences pose a problem for Black swimmers. Heavier skeletons and smaller chest cavities limit their performance.

Race differences show up early in life. Black babies are born a week earlier than White babies, yet they are more mature as measured by bone development. By age five or six, Black children excel in the dash, the long jump, and the high jump, all of which require a short burst of power. By the teenage years, Blacks have faster reflexes, as in the famous knee-jerk response.

East Asians run even less well than Whites. The same narrow hips, longer legs, more muscle, and more testosterone that give Blacks an advantage over Whites, give Whites an advantage over East Asians. But admitting these genetic race differences in sports leads to the greater taboo area — race differences in brain size and crime. That is why it is taboo to even say that Blacks are better at many sports.

The reason why Whites and East Asians have wider hips than Blacks, and so make poorer runners is because they give birth to larger brained babies. During evolution, increasing cranial size meant women had to have a wider pelvis. Further, the hormones that give Blacks an edge at sports makes them restless in school and prone to crime.

Race in History

Even before there were any intelligence tests, philosophers, statesmen, merchants, and others thought there was a link between race, intelligence, and cultural achievement. Aristotle, Plato, Voltaire, and David Hume all believed this. So did Broca, Darwin, Galton, and all the founders of evolution and anthropology. Even Freud believed in some race differences. But this began to change in the 1920s with Franz Boas and James B. Watson, who believed that culture could change just about anything. Today, writers like Jared Diamond in *Guns, Germs and Steel* (1997) and S. J. Gould in *The Mismeasure of Man* (1996) tell us there is no link between race, intelligence, and culture. The differences we see are all just because of bad luck or White racism.

The first explorers in East Africa wrote that they were shocked by the nudity, paganism, cannibalism, and poverty of the natives. Some claimed Blacks had the nature "of wild animals... most of them go naked... the child does not know his father, and they eat people." Another claimed they had a natural sense of rhythm so that if a Black "were to fall from heaven to earth he would beat time as he goes down." A few even wrote books and made paintings of Africans with over-sized sex organs.

Sound familiar? All just a reflection of racism? Maybe so, but these examples are not from 19th Century European colonialists or KKK hate literature. They come from the Muslim Arabs who first entered Black Africa over 1,200 years ago (in the 700s), as detailed in Bernard Lewis's 1990 book, *Race and Slavery in the Middle East*.

Several hundred years later, European explorers had the same impressions. They wrote that Africans seemed to have a very low intelligence and few words to express complex thoughts. They praised some tribes for making fine pottery, forging iron, carving wooden art, and making musical instruments. But more often, they were shocked by the near nakedness of the people, their poor sanitary habits, simple houses, and small villages. They found no wheels for making pots, grinding corn, or for transport, no farm animals, no writing, no money, and no numbering systems.

The Whites who explored China were just as racist as those who explored Africa, but their descriptions were different from what they and the Arabs had written about Africans. In 1275 Marco Polo arrived in China from his native Italy to open trade with the Mongol Empire. He found that the Chinese had well built roads, bridges, cities connected by canals, census takers, markets, standardized weights and measures, and not only coins, but paper money as well. Even a postal system was in existence. All of these made him marvel when he compared the Chinese to what he saw in Europe and the Middle East. Even though he was an Italian, proud of his people and well aware of the greatness of Ancient Rome, Marco Polo wrote: "Surely there is no more intelligent race on earth than the Chinese."

Historical research bears out Marco Polo's impressions. As early as 360 B.C., the Chinese used the cross bow and changed the face of warfare. Around 200-100 B.C., the Chinese used written exams to choose people for the civil service, two thousand years before

Britain. The Chinese used printing about 800 A.D., some 600 years before Europe saw Gutenberg's first Bible. Paper money was used in China in 1300, but not in Europe until the 19th and 20th centuries. By 1050 Chinese chemists had made gunpowder, hand grenades, fire arrows, and rockets of oil and poison gas. By 1100, factories in China with 40,000 workers were making rockets. Flame throwers, guns, and cannons were used in China by the 13th century, about 100 years before Europe.

The Chinese used the magnetic compass as early as the 1st century. It is not found in European records until 1190. In 1422, seventy years before Columbus's three small ships crossed the Atlantic, the Chinese reached the east coast of Africa. They came in a great fleet of 65 ocean going ships filled with 27,000 soldiers and their horses, and a year's supply of grain, meat, and wine. With their gunpowder weapons, navigation, accurate maps and magnetic compasses, the Chinese could easily have gone around the tip of Africa and "discovered" Europe!

In the last five centuries, the European nations leapfrogged over the Chinese in science and technology. Since 1950, however, Japan has beaten the West in the production of many high-tech products. Other Pacific Rim countries (China, Taiwan, Singapore, and South Korea) now follow Japan's path.

Africa, on the other hand, has fallen further behind. The poor conditions of African countries and Black America have become a concern to many. Much of the optimism of the U.S. Civil Rights movement of the 1960s is gone, along with the high hopes for independent African nations. Trillions of dollars of foreign aid have poured into Africa. Yet African economies have declined since the Europeans left.

Neglect and decay are seen everywhere in Africa and much of the West Indies. International corporations often have to provide their own power, their own water, and their own phones. In the age of computers, fax machines, and the world wide web, getting a dial tone in many African cities is difficult.

Race in Today's World

For the past twenty years I have studied race differences in brain size, intelligence, sexuality, personality, growth rate, life span, crime, and family stability. On all of these traits, Orientals fall at one end of the spectrum, Blacks fall at the other end, and Whites fall in between.

Chart 1 lists the differences between the three major races: *Orientals* (East Asians, Mongoloids), *Whites* (Europeans, Caucasoids), and *Blacks* (Africans, Negroids). To keep things simple, I will use these common names instead of scientific ones and will not discuss subgroups within the races.

On average, Orientals are slower to mature, less fertile, and less sexually active, have larger brains and higher IQ scores. Blacks are at the opposite end in each of these areas. Whites fall in the middle, often close to Orientals. The evidence shows that this is due to both

Chart 1

Average Differences Among Blacks, Whites, and Orientals

Trait	Blacks	Whites	Orientals
Brain Size:			
Cranial capacity	1,267	1,347	1,364
Cortical neurons (millions)	13,185	13,665	13,767
Intelligence:			
IQ test scores	85	100	106
Cultural achievements	Low	High	High
Reproduction:			
2-egg twinning (per 1000 births)	16	8	4
Hormone levels	Higher	Intermediate	Lower
Sex characteristics	Larger	Intermediate	Smaller
Intercourse frequencies	Higher	Intermediate	Lower
Permissive attitudes	Higher	Intermediate	Lower
Sexually transmitted diseases	Higher	Intermediate	Lower
Personality:			
Aggressiveness	Higher	Intermediate	Lower
Cautiousness	Lower	Intermediate	Higher
Impulsivity	Higher	Intermediate	Lower
Self-concept	Higher	Intermediate	Lower
Sociability	Higher	Intermediate	Lower
Maturation:			
Gestation time	Shorter	Longer	Longer
Skeletal development	Earlier	Intermediate	Later
Motor development	Earlier	Intermediate	Later
Dental development	Earlier	Intermediate	Later
Age of first intercourse	Earlier	Intermediate	Later
Age of first pregnancy	Earlier	Intermediate	Later
Life-span	Shortest	Intermediate	Longest
Social organization:			
Marital stability	Lower	Intermediate	Higher
Law abidingness	Lower	Intermediate	Higher
Mental health	Low	Intermediate	Higher

Source: Unabridged edition, *Race, Evolution, and Behavior* (p. 5).

genes and environment. I have suggested an evolutionary theory to explain this three-way pattern.

Of course, these differences are *averages*. The full range of behaviors, good and bad, is found in every race. No group has a monopoly on virtue or vice, wisdom or folly. However, this pattern is true over time and across nations and this means that we cannot ignore it.

Plan of the Book

This chapter briefly describes the 3-way pattern of race differences. The following chapters provide more detail.

Many statistics in Chart 1 come from the United States, where Orientals are a "model minority." They have fewer divorces, fewer out-of-wedlock births, and fewer reports of child abuse than Whites.   More Orientals graduate from college and fewer go to prison.

On the other hand Blacks are 12% of the American population and make up 50% of the prison population. In the U.S., one out of every three Black men is either in jail, on probation, or awaiting trial. That is much more than the number who graduate from college.

Chapter 2 shows how this racial pattern in crime is found worldwide. INTERPOL Yearbooks show the rate of violent crime (murder, rape, and serious assault) is four times lower in Asian and Pacific Rim countries than in African and Caribbean countries. Whites in the United States and in European countries are intermediate. The 1996 INTERPOL violent crime rates clearly show this pattern: Asian countries, 35 violent crimes per 100,000 people; European countries, 42; and African countries, 149.

Chapter 2 also finds that Oriental children are slower to mature than White children while Black children are faster to mature. This is true for the rate of bone and tooth development and the age at which a child first sits, crawls, walks, and puts on clothing. Oriental children do not begin to walk until about 13 months, White children at 12 months, and Black children at 11 months.

Chapter 3 looks at racial differences in sexual activity. Orientals are the least sexually active, whether measured by age of first intercourse, intercourse frequency, or number of sexual partners. Blacks are the most active on all of these. Once again Whites are in between. These contrasts in sexual activity lead to differences in the rate of diseases like syphilis, gonorrhea, herpes, and chlamydia. There are high levels of AIDS in Africa, Black America, and the Caribbean and low levels in China and Japan. European countries again fall in between.

The races differ in rate of ovulation (Chapter 3). Not all women produce one egg during the menstrual cycle. When two or more eggs are produced at the same time, a pregnancy is more likely. So is the likelihood of producing fraternal twins (i.e., two-egg twins). The number of twins born is 16 out of every 1,000 births for Blacks, 8 out of every 1,000 births for Whites, and 4 or less for Orientals. Triplets and other multiple births are rarest in Orientals and highest in Blacks, with Whites in between.

Chapter 4 is about race and intelligence. Hundreds of studies on millions of people show a three-way pattern. IQ tests are often made to have an average score of 100, with a "normal" range from 85 to 115. Whites average from 100 to 103. Orientals in Asia and the U.S. tend to have higher scores, about 106, even though IQ tests were made for use in the Euro-American culture. Blacks in the U.S., the Caribbean, Britain, Canada, and in Africa average lower IQs -- about 85. The lowest average IQs are found for sub-Saharan Africans -- from 70 to 75.

Chapter 4 also looks at brain size. Bigger brains have more brain cells and this leads to higher IQs. The races vary in brain size. The Collaborative Perinatal Project followed more than 35,000 children from birth to seven years. Orientals had larger brains than Whites at birth, four months, one year, and seven years. Whites had larger brains than Blacks at all ages (see Chart 2). The data on adults in Chart 2 come from a sample of 6,325 U.S. Army personnel.

Chapter 5 asks whether differences in our brain size, our bodies and our behavior are because of genes, environment, or both. It also asks whether individual differences can tell us anything about race differences.

Why Are There Race Differences?

Why does history show Africa trailing behind Asia and Europe? Why do Whites average *between* Orientals and Blacks in so many areas? Why do the groups with larger brains have lower rates of two-egg twinning? To know the answer you must look at all of the traits taken together (see Chart 1).

Chart 2

**Average Cranial Size for Blacks, Whites, and Orientals
in the U.S. at 5 Different Ages**

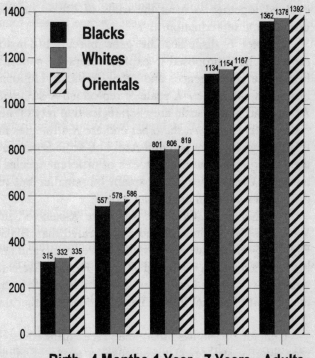

Cranial capacity in cubic centimeters. Birth through age 7 from
U.S. Perinatal Project; Adults from U.S. Army. From J.P. Rushton,
1997, *Intelligence*, 25, p. 15.

The traits in Chart 1 form a pattern. *No known environmental factor can explain all of them taken together.* There is, however, a gene based explanation. The patterns make up what is called a "life-history." They evolved together to meet the trials of life -- survival, growth, and reproduction.

Chapter 6 discusses the gene based "life-history theory" I have proposed to explain the racial pattern in brain size, intelligence, and other traits. Evolutionary biologists call it the *r-K* scale of reproductive strategies. At one end of this scale are *r*-strategies that rely on high reproductive rates. At the other end are *K*-strategies that rely on high levels of parental care. This scale is generally used to compare the life histories of different species of animals. I have used it to explain the smaller but real differences between the human races.

On this scale, Orientals are more *K*-selected than Whites, while Whites are more *K*-selected than Blacks. Highly *K*-selected women produce fewer eggs (and have bigger brains) than *r*-selected women. Highly *K*-selected men invest time and energy in their children rather than the pursuit of sexual thrills. They are "dads" rather than "cads."

Chapter 7 shows that the race differences in reproductive strategies make sense in terms of human evolution. Modern humans evolved in Africa about 200,000 years ago. Africans and non-Africans then split about 100,000 years ago. Orientals and Whites split about 40,000 years ago.

The more north the people went "Out of Africa," the harder it was to get food, gain shelter, make clothes, and raise children. So the groups that evolved into today's Whites and Orientals needed larger brains, more family stability, and a longer life. But building a bigger brain takes time and energy during a person's development. So, these changes were balanced by slower rates of growth, lower levels of sex hormones, less aggression, and less sexual activity.

Why? Because Africa, Europe, and Asia had very different climates and geographies that called for different skills, resource usage, and lifestyles. Blacks evolved in a tropical climate which contrasted with the cooler one of Europe in which Whites evolved and even more so with the cold Arctic lands where Orientals evolved.

Because intelligence increased the chances of survival in harsh winter environments, the groups that left Africa had to evolve greater intelligence and family stability. This called for larger brains, slower growth rates, lower hormone levels, less sexual potency, less aggression, and less impulsivity. Advanced planning, self-control, rule-following, and longevity all increased in the non-Africans.

I realize that these topics are controversial and that readers will have many questions. Chapter 8 lists the questions I am most asked about *Race, Evolution, and Behavior*, and my answers to them.

Conclusion

Race is more than "just skin deep." The pattern of Oriental-White-Black differences is found across history, geographic boundaries, and political-economic systems. It proves the biological reality of race. Theories based only on culture cannot explain all the data shown in Chart 1. The next three chapters describe the scientific findings on race differences (summarized in Chart 1) in greater detail. Later chapters explain why these differences follow such a pattern.

Additional Readings

Entine, J. (2000). *Taboo: Why Black Athletes Dominate Sports and Why We Are Afraid to Talk About It.* New York: Public Affairs Press.

Lewis, B. (1990). *Race and Slavery in the Middle East.* New York: Oxford University Press.

Rushton, J. P. (1997). Cranial size and IQ in Asian Americans from birth to age seven. *Intelligence, 25,* 7-20.

2

Maturation, Crime, and Parenting

*Race differences start in the womb.
Blacks are born earlier and grow quicker
than Whites and Orientals. The three-way
race pattern occurs in milestones such as
sexual maturity, family stability, crime
rates, and population growth.*

Black babies mature more quickly than White babies, while Oriental babies mature more slowly. African babies in a sitting position are more able to keep their heads up and backs straight from the start. White babies often need six to eight *weeks* to do these things (see Chart 3). It is unlikely that social factors could produce these differences. A basic law of biology shows that longer infancy is related to greater brain growth (see Chapter 6).

These differences in growth rate mean that races tend to differ in the age when they reach milestones such as the end of infancy, the start of puberty, adulthood, and old age. The races also differ in crime rates, parenting style, and even population growth.

Chart 3

Black Infants Develop Physically Sooner than Other Infants

Two days old, holding head and looking at examiner (White child, eight weeks)

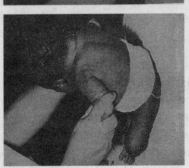

Nine hours old, able to keep the head from falling backwards (White child, six weeks)

Source: Geber, M. (1958). *Journal of Social Psychology, 47*, 185-195.

Maturation

Black babies spend the least time in the womb. In America, 51% of Black children have been born by week 39 of pregnancy compared with 33% of White children. In Europe, Black babies of even professional mothers are born earlier than White babies.

These Black babies are not born premature. They are born sooner, but biologically they are more mature. The length of pregnancy depends on the genes.

The faster pace of growth among Blacks goes on through childhood. Black babies have greater muscular strength and can reach for objects better. Their neck muscles are often so developed that they can lift their heads up when they are only nine hours old. In a matter of days they can turn themselves over.

Black children sit, crawl, walk, and put on their own clothes earlier than Whites or Orientals. The findings are measured by such tests as Bayley's Scales of Mental and Motor Development and the Cambridge Neonatal Scales.

Oriental children, on the other hand, mature more slowly than do White children. Oriental children often do not walk until 13 months. Walking starts at 12 months for White children and 11 months for Black children.

X-rays show bones grow faster in Black children than in White children. Whites develop bones faster than Orientals. Brain wave patterns develop faster in Black than in White newborns.

Blacks have faster dental development than Whites, who mature faster than Orientals. Black children begin the first part of permanent tooth growth at about 5.8 years and finish at 7.6 years. Whites begin at 6.1 years and finish at 7.7 years, while Orientals begin at 6.1 years and finish at 7.8 years. Blacks have larger jaws and larger teeth. They have more teeth and more often have the third and fourth molars. Whites have larger jaws and teeth and more teeth than do Orientals.

Blacks reach sexual maturity sooner than Whites, who in turn mature sooner than Orientals. This is true for things like age at first menstruation, first sexual experience, and first pregnancy.

One study of over 17,000 American girls in the 1997 issue of *Pediatrics* found that puberty begins a year earlier for Black girls than for White girls. By age eight, 48% of the Black girls (but only 15% of the White girls) had some breast development, pubic hair, or both. For Whites this did not happen until ten years. The age when girls began to menstruate was between 11 and 12 for Black girls. White girls began a year later.

Sexual maturity in boys also differs by race. By age 11, 60% of Black boys have reached the stage of puberty marked by fast penis growth. Two percent have already had sex. White boys tend not to reach this stage for another 1.5 years. Orientals lag one to two years behind Whites in both sexual development and the start of sexual interest.

Crime

In the U.S., Blacks are less than 13% of the population but have 50% of all arrests for assault and murder and 67% of all arrests for robbery. Fifty percent of all crime victims also report their assailants are Black, so the arrest statistics cannot be due to police bias.

Blacks make up a large share of those arrested for white-collar crimes. About 33% of persons arrested for fraud, forgery, counterfeiting, and receiving stolen property, and about 25% of those arrested for embezzlement are Black. Blacks are under-represented only in offenses, such as tax fraud and securities violations, that are committed by individuals in high status occupations.

On the other hand, Orientals are under-represented in U.S. crime statistics. This has led some to argue that the Asian "ghetto" has protected members from harmful outside influences. For Blacks, however, the ghetto is said to foster crime, so purely cultural explanations are not enough.

Female homicides tell the same story. In one study of female arrests, 75% were Black women. Only 13% were White women. No Asian women were arrested. The cultural explanation for the crime rate of Black men does not apply to Black women, who are not expected to engage in criminal behavior to the same extent. There is no "gangster" image among Black females.

The same pattern is found in other countries. In London, England, Blacks make up 13% of the population, but account for 50% of the crime rate. A 1996 government commission in Ontario, Canada, reported that Blacks were five times more likely go to jail than Whites, and 10 times more likely than Orientals. In Brazil, there are 1.5 million Orientals, mostly Japanese whose ancestors went there as laborers in the 19th century, and who are the least represented in crime.

Chart 4 is based on INTERPOL Yearbooks and shows that this racial pattern is consistent globally. Rates of murder, rape, and serious assault were four times higher in African and Caribbean countries than in Asian or Pacific Rim countries. European countries were intermediate. The 1993-1996 INTERPOL Yearbooks show the violent crime rate per 100,000 population was 35 for Asians, 42 for Europeans, and 149 for Africans.

Personality, Aggression, and Self-Esteem

Studies find that Blacks are more aggressive and outgoing than Whites, while Whites are more aggressive and outgoing than Orientals. Blacks also have more mental instability than Whites. Black rates of drug and alcohol abuse are higher. Again, Orientals are under-represented in mental health statistics.

A study carried out in French-speaking Quebec looked at 825 four- to six-year-olds from 66 countries. The immigrant children were rated by 50 teachers in preschool classes. The teachers found more adjustment and less hostility among Oriental children than among White children, but they also saw more adjustment and less hostility among White children than among Black children.

Chart 4

INTERPOL Crime Rates for the Three Races
(Murder, Rape, and Serious Assault)
per 100,000 Population

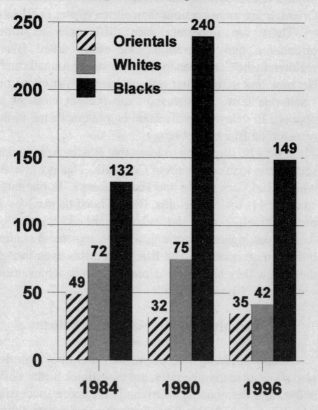

Source: Third Unabridged Edition of *Race Evolution, and Behavior*
(pp. P-24, 159, 287).

Racial differences in personality are found using tests such as the Eysenck Personality Questionnaire and Cattell's Sixteen Personality Factor Questionnaire. Orientals everywhere are less aggressive, dominant, and impulsive than Whites and Whites are less so than Blacks. Orientals are more cautious than either Whites or Blacks.

There are important race differences in time-orientation and motivation. One study asked Black children in the Caribbean to choose between a small candy bar now and a larger bar a week later. Most chose the small one now. A focus on the present moment as opposed to delayed gratification is a major theme in the research on Black psychology.

It may be surprising to learn that Blacks have higher self esteem than do Whites or Orientals. This is true even when Blacks are poorer and less educated. In one large study of 11- to 16-year-olds, Blacks rated themselves as more attractive than did Whites. Blacks also rated themselves higher in reading, science and social studies but not mathematics. The Blacks said this even though they knew they had lower *actual* academic achievement scores than White children.

Parenting and Out-of-Wedlock Births

Racial differences in personality and obeying rules also show up in divorce rates, out of wedlock births, child abuse, and delinquency. Orientals are more successful than Whites or Blacks. They have fewer divorces, fewer out of wedlock births, and less child abuse than Whites.

On the other hand, Black family stability is a concern. In 1965 the Moynihan Report showed the higher rates of marital breakup, female headed families, and out of wedlock births among Blacks. Since then the figures have tripled! About 75% of births to Black teenagers are out of wedlock, compared with 25% of White teenagers.

The female-headed family is not unique to the U.S. Nor is it the result of the legacy of slavery or inner city decay. It is found in large areas of Black Africa.

In Africa, the female-headed family is part of an overall social pattern. It consists of early sexual activity, loose emotional ties between spouses and sexual union and the procreation of children with many partners. It includes fostering children away from home, even for several years, so mothers remain sexually attractive. Males likewise compete more for females and fathers are less involved in child rearing.

Compared to others in poor countries, African women stop breastfeeding their children early. This allows ovulation to resume, so mothers conceive again, thus producing a higher birth rate. Once a child is about a year old, other children and grandparents do much of the caretaking. As children grow older, they look to older children for basic needs. In Black Africa and the Black Caribbean, as in the American underclass ghetto, groups of pre-teens and teenagers are left quite free of adult supervision.

Longevity and Population Growth

Death rates show the same pattern of racial differences. Blacks have more disease and a higher death rate at every age. Orientals have the lowest death rate and outlive Whites by two years, about as long as Whites outlive Blacks.

Black American babies are twice as likely to die in infancy as White babies. Single parenting, poverty, or lack of education, however, are not the only causes. One study of college graduates with access to good medical care shows a death rate that is still twice as high among Black infants as among White infants.

Mortality differences continue into adulthood. In one U.S. Navy study, Blacks had higher rates of accidental and violent deaths from all causes. Another study revealed Blacks had higher rates of death in auto accidents.

This is a global pattern. East Asian countries like Japan and Singapore have lower death rates than European countries. European countries have lower death rates than African and Black Caribbean countries. But, the pattern for suicide is reversed. East Asian countries have the highest rates, about 15 suicides per 100,000 people. European rates are about 12 per 100,000, while African and Caribbean countries have the lowest rates of about 4 per 100,000.

A higher birth rate more than makes up for the shorter Black life span. Africa's population growth has been a concern. It is 3.2% a year. The highest rate in the world! South Asia and Latin America growth rates of 2.1% and 2.5% have reduced population increase since 1960. In the

U.S. the average woman will have 14 descendants including children, grandchildren, and great-grandchildren. An average African woman will have 258. The African continent accounted for 9% of the world's population in 1950. Despite AIDS, warfare, disease, drought and famine, Africa has grown to be 12% of the world's population today.

Conclusion

The three-way pattern of race differences is true for growth rates, life span, personality, family functioning, criminality, and success in social organization. Black babies mature faster than White babies; Oriental babies mature slower than Whites. The same pattern is true for sexual maturity, out of wedlock births, and even child abuse. Around the world, Blacks have the highest crime rate, Orientals the least, Whites fall in between. The same pattern is true for personality. Blacks are the most outgoing and even have the highest self-esteem. Orientals are the most willing to delay gratification. Whites fall in between. Blacks die earliest, Whites next, Orientals last, even when all have good medical care. The three-way racial pattern holds up from cradle to grave.

Additional Readings

Herman-Giddens, M. E., and others. (1997). Secondary sexual characteristics and menses in young girls seen in the office practice. *Pediatrics, 99*, 505-512.

Rushton, J. P. (1995). Race and crime: International data for 1989-1990. *Psychological Reports, 76,* 307-312.

3

Sex, Hormones, and AIDS

Race differences exist in sexual behavior. The races differ in how often they like to have sexual intercourse. This affects rates of sexually transmitted diseases. On all the counts, Orientals are the least sexually active, Blacks the most, and Whites are in between. The races also differ in the number of twins and multiple births, in hormone levels, in sexual attitudes, and even in their sexual anatomy.

The races differ in their level of sex hormones. Hormone levels are highest in Blacks and the lowest in Orientals. This may tell us why Black women have premenstrual syndrome (PMS) the most and Orientals the least.

The races also differ in testosterone level which helps to explain men's behavior. In one study of college students, testosterone levels were 10 to 20% higher in Blacks than in Whites. For an older sample of U.S. military veterans, Blacks had levels 3% higher than Whites (see the 1992 issue of *Steroids*). In a study of university students, Black

Americans had 10 to 15% higher levels than White Americans. The Japanese (in Japan) had even lower levels.

Testosterone acts as a "master switch." It affects things like self-concept, aggression, altruism, crime, and sexuality, not just in men, but in women too. Testosterone also controls things like muscle mass and the deepening of the voice in the teenage years.

Sexual Behavior and Attitudes

Blacks are sexually active at an earlier age than Whites. Whites, in turn, are sexually active earlier than Orientals. Surveys from the World Health Organization show this three-way racial pattern to be true around the world. National surveys from Britain and the United States produce the same findings.

A Los Angeles study found that the age of first sexual activity in high school students was 16.4 years for Orientals, 14.4 years for Blacks, with Whites in the middle. The percentage of students who were sexually active was 32% for Orientals but 81% for Blacks. Whites again fell between the two other races. A Canadian study found Orientals to be more restrained, even in fantasy and masturbation. Orientals born in Canada were just as restrained as recent Asian immigrants.

Around the world, sexual activity for married couples follows the three way pattern. A 1951 survey asked people how often they had sex. Pacific Islanders and Native Americans said from 1 to 4 times per week, U.S. Whites answered 2 to 4 times per week, while Africans said they had sex 3 to 10 times per week. Later surveys have confirmed these findings. The average frequency of intercourse per week for married couples in their twenties is 2.5 for the Japanese and Chinese in Asia. It is 4 for American Whites. For American Blacks it is 5.

Racial differences are found in sexual permissiveness, thinking about sex, and even in levels of sex guilt. In one study, three generations of Japanese Americans and Japanese students in Japan had less interest in sex than European students. Yet each generation of Japanese Americans had more sex guilt than White Americans their age. In another study, British men and women said they had three times as many sexual fantasies as Japanese men and women. Orientals were the most likely to say that sex has a weakening effect. Blacks said they had casual intercourse more and felt less concern about it than Whites did.

Sexual Physiology and Anatomy

Ovulation rates differ by race, as does the frequency of twins. Black women tend to have shorter cycles than do White women. They often produce two eggs in a single cycle. This makes them more fertile.

The rate of two-egg twins is less than 4 in every 1,000 births for Orientals. It is 8 for Whites, but for Blacks it is 16 or greater. Triplets and quadruplets are very rare in all groups, but they show the same three-way order -- Blacks have the most, then Whites, and Orientals the least.

From the 8th to the 16th centuries, Arab Islamic literature showed Black Africans, both men and women, as having high sexual potency and large organs.

Nineteenth century European anthropologists reported on the position of female genitals (Orientals highest, Blacks lowest, Whites intermediate) and the angle of the male erection (Orientals parallel to the body, Blacks at right angles). They claimed Orientals also had the least secondary sex characteristics (visible muscles, buttocks, and breasts), Blacks the most. Other early anthropologists also reported that people of mixed race tended to fall in between.

Should we take these early reports by outsiders on so sensitive a subject seriously? Modern data seem to confirm these early observations. Around the world, public health agencies now give out free condoms to help slow the spread of AIDS and help save lives. Condom size can affect whether one is used, so these agencies take note of penis size when they give out condoms. The World Health Organization Guidelines specify a 49-mm-width condom for Asia, a 52-mm-width for North America and Europe, and a 53-mm-width for Africa. China is now making its own condoms -- 49 mm.

Race differences in testicle size have also been measured (Asians = 9 grams, Europeans = 21 g). This is not just because Europeans have a slightly larger body size. The difference is too large. A 1989 article in *Nature,* the leading British science magazine, said that the difference in testicle size could mean that Whites make two times as many sperm per day as do Orientals. So far, we have no information on the relative size of Blacks.

AIDS and HIV

Race differences in sexual behavior have results in real life. They affect sexually transmitted disease rates. The World Health Organization takes note of sexual diseases like syphilis, gonorrhea, herpes and chlamydia. They report low levels in China and Japan and high levels in Africa. European countries are in the middle.

The racial pattern of these diseases is also true in the U.S. The 1997 syphilis rate among Blacks was 24 times the White rate. The nationwide syphilis rate for Blacks was 22 cases per 100,000 people. It was 0.5 cases per 100,000 for Whites, and even lower for Orientals. A recent report found up to 25% of inner city girls (mainly Black) have chlamydia.

Racial differences also show in the current AIDS crisis. Over 30 million people around the world are living with HIV or AIDS. Many Blacks in the U.S. do get AIDS through drug use, but more get it through sex. At the other extreme, more AIDS sufferers in China and Japan are hemophiliacs. European countries have intermediate HIV infection rates, mostly among homosexual men.

Chart 5 shows the yearly estimates of the HIV infection rate in various parts of the world from the United Nations. The epidemic started in Black Africa in the late 1970s. Today 23 million adults there are living with HIV/AIDS. Over fifty percent of these are female. This shows that transmission is mainly heterosexual. Currently, 8 out of every 100 Africans are infected with the AIDS virus and the epidemic is considered out of control. In

Chart 5

HIV/AIDS Rates (%) for 15 to 49 year olds in 1999

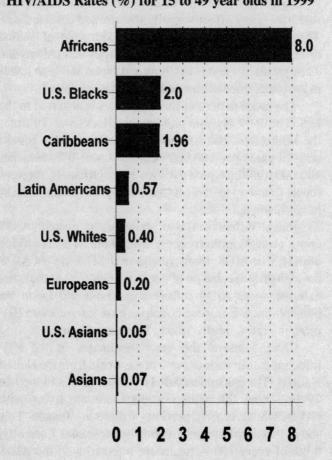

some areas the AIDS rate reaches 70%. In South Africa one in 10 adults is living with HIV.

The HIV infection rate is also high in the Black Caribbean. About 2%! Thirty-three percent of the AIDS cases there are women. This high figure among women shows that the spread tends to be from heterosexual intercourse. The high rate of HIV in the 2,000 mile band of Caribbean countries extends from Bermuda to Guyana, and it seems to be the highest in Haiti, with a rate close to 6%. It is the most infected area outside of Black Africa.

Data published by the U.S. Centers for Disease Control and Prevention show that African Americans have HIV rates similar to the Black Caribbean and parts of Black Africa. Three percent of Black men and 1% of Black women in the U.S. are living with HIV (Chart 5). The rate for White Americans is less than 0.1%, while the rate for Asian Americans is less than 0.05%. Rates for Europe and the Pacific Rim are also low. Of course AIDS is a serious public health problem for all racial groups, but it is especially so for Africans and people of African descent.

Conclusion

The three-way pattern of race differences is found in rates of multiple births (two-egg twinning), hormone levels, sexual attitudes, sexual anatomy, frequency of intercourse, and sexually transmitted diseases (STDs). Both male and female sex hormone levels are the highest in Blacks, the lowest in Orientals, with Whites in between. Sex hormones affect not only our bodies, but also the way we act and think. Blacks are the most sexually active, have the most multiple births, and have the most permissive attitudes. Orientals are the least sexually active and show the least sexual fantasy and the most sexual guilt. Whites are in the middle. Sex diseases are most common in Blacks, least so in Orientals, with Whites in between the two. The very high rate of AIDS in Africa, the Black Caribbean and in Black Americans is alarming.

Additional Readings

Ellis, L., & Nyborg, H. (1992). Racial/ethnic variations in male testosterone levels: A probable contributor to group differences in health. *Steroids*, *57*, 72-75.

UNAIDS (1999). *AIDS epidemic update: December 1999*. United Nations Program on HIV/AIDS. New York.

4

Intelligence and Brain Size

*IQ tests measure intelligence and predict
real life success. The races differ in brain
size and on IQ tests. On average Orientals
have the largest brains and highest IQs.
Blacks average the lowest, and Whites fall
in between. The brain size differences
explain the IQ differences both within
groups and between groups.*

Psychologists use IQ tests to measure what we call
"intelligence" or "mental ability." Brighter people score
higher on IQ tests than most people. Less bright people
score lower. IQ tests are not perfect, but they are useful
and tell us a lot.

IQ tests are made to have an average of 100. The
"normal" range goes from "dull" (IQ around 85) to
"bright" (IQ around 115). IQs of 70 suggest handicap,
while IQs of 130 and above predict giftedness. The
average Oriental IQ is about 106, the White IQ about 100,
and the Black IQ about 85. This pattern is found around
the world, with Blacks in Africa having a lower IQ than
Blacks in America.

The 1994 best seller *The Bell Curve* shows how IQ predicts success in education, jobs, and training. Low IQ predicts child abuse, crime and delinquency, health, accident proneness, having a child out of wedlock, getting a divorce before five years of marriage, and even smoking during pregnancy. Groups with higher IQs have more gifted people. While Orientals developed complex societies in Asia, and Whites produced complex civilizations in Europe, Black Africans did not.

The Black-White difference in IQ appears as early as three years of age. If the races are matched for education and income, the gap only goes down by 4 IQ points. So, Black-White differences are not due only to social class. It is less well known that Orientals have a higher IQ than Whites.

The Bell Curve highlighted British psychologist Richard Lynn's 20 year survey of the global pattern of IQ scores. He found Orientals in the Pacific Rim to have IQs in the 101 to 111 range, Whites in Europe to have IQs of 100 to 103, and Blacks in Africa to have IQs of around 70 (see Chart 6).

The average IQ of 70 for Blacks living in Africa is the lowest ever recorded. The Raven's Progressive Matrices measures reasoning, not culturally specific information. Using this test, Kenneth Owen found a Black African IQ of 70 for 13-year-olds in the South African school system. So did Fred Zindi, a Black Zimbabwean, in a study of 12- to 14-year-olds in his country.

Chart 6

Average IQ Scores for the Various Races

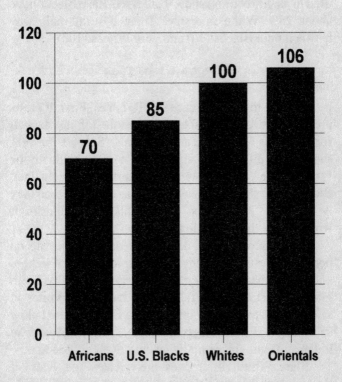

Source: Third Unabridged Edition of *Race, Evolution, and Behavior* (pp. P-15 to P-16, 135-137, 278-280).

Interestingly, the Mixed-Race students in South Africa had an IQ of 85 -- the same as Blacks in the United States, Britain, and the Caribbean. Genetic methods (like those used in paternity tests) show that Mixed-Race Blacks have about 25% White ancestry. Their IQs fall half way between pure Blacks (70) and pure Whites (100).

Culture Fair Tests

Is it fair to compare race and IQ? Yes. First, IQ tests predict achievement in school and on the job just as well for Blacks as for Whites and Orientals. Second, the very same race differences show up on tests made to be "culture-free" as well as on standard IQ tests. In fact, Blacks score slightly *higher* on standard IQ tests than they do on these "culture-free" tests. This is the opposite of what culture theory predicts.

Blacks score higher on verbal tests than they do on nonverbal tests, and they do better on tests of school knowledge than they do on tests of reasoning ability. From grades 1 to 12, Blacks fall just as far below Whites in school work as they do on IQ tests. Blacks score below even more disadvantaged groups, such as American Indians. Again, this is not what culture theory predicts.

Black-White differences are greatest on tests of reasoning and logic. Blacks do best on tests of simple memory. For example, Blacks do almost as well as Whites on tests of Forward Digit Span, in which people repeat a series of digits in the same order as they have heard them. Blacks do much poorer than Whites, however, on tests of Backward Digit Span, in which people repeat the digits back in reverse order. Hundreds of studies reviewed in Arthur Jensen's book *The g Factor* show how hard it is to explain race differences in IQ just in terms of cultural bias.

Probably reaction time is the simplest culture free mental test. In the "odd-man-out" test, 9- to 12-year-old children look at a set of lights. They have to decide which one goes on, and then press the button closest to that light. The test is so easy that all children can do it in less than one second. Even here, children with higher IQ scores are faster than lower IQ children. Around the world, Oriental children are faster than White children who are faster than Black children.

Intelligence and Brain Size

My article with C. D. Ankney "Brain Size and Cognitive Ability" in the 1996 issue of the journal *Psychonomic Bulletin and Review* surveyed all the published research on this topic. It included studies that used the state-of-the-art technique known as Magnetic Resonance Imaging (MRI) which gives a very good image of the human brain. There were eight of these studies with a total sample size of 381 adults. The overall correlation between IQ and brain size measured by MRI is 0.44. This is much higher than the 0.20 correlation found in earlier research using simple head size measures (though 0.20 is still significant). The MRI brain size/IQ correlation of 0.44 is as high as the correlation between social class at birth and adult IQ.

Race Differences in Brain Size

Chart 7 shows that there are race differences in brain size. Orientals average 1 cubic inch more brain matter than Whites, and Whites average a very large 5 cubic inches more than Blacks. Since one cubic inch of brain matter contains millions of brain cells and hundreds of millions of connections, brain size differences help to explain why the races differ in IQ.

The rest of this chapter documents that four different methods used to measure brain size all produce the same results. The methods are MRI, weighing the brain at autopsy, measuring the volume of an empty skull, and measuring the outside of the head. Note that race differences in brain size remain even after you adjust for body size.

Magnetic Resonance Imaging

One MRI study of race differences in brain size looked at over 100 people in Britain. (It was published in the 1994 issue of *Psychological Medicine*). The Black Africans and West Indians in the study averaged smaller brains than did the Whites. Unfortunately, the study did not give much information on the age, sex, and body size of the people tested.

Chart 7

**Average Brain Size for the Three Races
(cm³)**

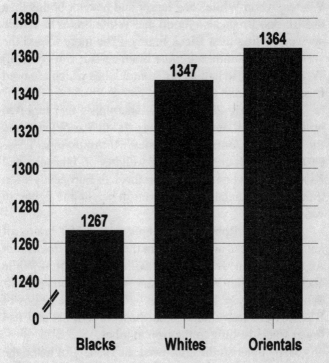

Source: Third Unabridged Edition of *Race, Evolution, and Behavior* (pp. P-13, 113-133, 282-284).

Brain Weight at Autopsy

In the 19th century, the famous neurologist Paul Broca found that Orientals had larger and heavier brains than did Whites, while Whites had larger and heavier brains than did Blacks. Broca also found that White brains had more surface folding than Black brains. (The more folded the surface of the brain, the more brain cells it can contain.) White brains also had larger frontal lobes which are used in self control and planning.

By the early 20th century, anatomists had reported brain weights at autopsy in journals such as *Science* and the *American Journal of Physical Anthropology*. These early studies found the brain weights of Japanese and Koreans were about the same as those of Europeans, even though the Orientals were shorter in height and lighter in weight.

In 1906, Robert Bean reported on 150 brains of autopsied Blacks and Whites in the *American Journal of Anatomy*. Brain weight varied with the amount of White ancestry from no White ancestry = 1,157 grams to half-White ancestry = 1,347 grams. He found the brains of Blacks were less folded than those of Whites and had fewer fibers leading to the frontal lobes.

Many other studies followed. In 1934, Vint noted the results of an autopsy study of brain weights from Black Africans in the *Journal of Anatomy*. He found that the brains of Africans were 10% lighter than those of Whites. In the 1934 issue of *Science*, Raymond Pearl reviewed autopsy results from Black and White soldiers who had died in the American Civil War (1861-1865). He found the brains of Whites weighed about 100 grams more than the brains of Blacks. And among Blacks, Pearl also found that brain weight increased with the amount of White ancestry.

In a 1970 article in the *American Journal of Physical Anthropology*, Philip V. Tobias claimed that all these early studies were wrong. He said they ignored factors like "sex, body size, age of death, childhood nutrition, origin of sample, occupation, and cause of death." However, when I myself averaged all the data in Tobias's review, I found it still showed that Orientals and Whites have heavier brains than Blacks. Even Tobias finally had to agree that Orientals have "millions" more extra neurons than Whites who have "millions" more than Blacks.

In 1980, Kenneth Ho's team confirmed the Black-White differences. Their autopsy study was published in the *Archives of Pathology and Laboratory Medicine*. It avoided the possible errors claimed by Tobias. Original brain weight data for 1,261 American adults showed that Whites averaged 100 grams more brain weight than did Blacks. Because the Blacks in the study were similar in body size to the Whites, differences in body size do not explain away these race differences in brain size.

Measuring Skull Size

Another way to measure brain size is by filling skulls with packing material. In the 19th century, over 1,000 skulls were studied by American anthropologist Samuel George Morton. He found that Blacks had skulls about 5 cubic inches smaller than Whites.

In 1942, anatomist Katherine Simmons reported on over 2,000 skulls in the journal *Human Biology*. She confirmed Morton's earlier work finding that Whites have larger skulls than Blacks. Because the Blacks in her sample were taller than the Whites, the skull size differences could not be due to body size.

Kenneth Beals and his team further confirmed these findings in the 1984 issue of *Current Anthropology*. They reported the measurements of up to 20,000 skulls from around the world. Skull sizes varied with place of origin. Skulls from East Asia were 3 cubic inches larger than those from Europe which were 5 cubic inches larger than skulls from Africa.

Measuring Living Heads

Brain size can be measured by taking outside head measurements. These results confirm the findings based on the method of weighing brains and filling skulls.

I reported (in the journal *Intelligence*, 1992) on a sample of thousands of U.S. Army personnel. Even after correcting for body size, Orientals had a larger head size than Whites, who had a larger head size than Blacks (see Chart 2, page 23). In 1994, I reported (also in *Intelligence*) a study of tens of thousands of men and women collected by the International Labour Office in Geneva, Switzerland. Head sizes (corrected for body size) were larger for East Asians than for Europeans. Europeans had larger heads than Blacks.

In another study (in the 1997 issue of *Intelligence*), I reported the measurements for 35,000 children followed from birth to age 7 by the famous Collaborative Perinatal Study. At birth, four months, one year, and seven years, Oriental children had larger cranial sizes than White children, who had larger cranial sizes than Black children (see Chart 2, p. 23). These differences were not due to body size because the Black children were taller and heavier than the White and Oriental children.

Summarizing Brain Size Differences

Chart 7 shows average brain size for the three races using all four measurement techniques and also (where possible) correcting for body size. Orientals averaged 1,364 cm^3, Whites averaged 1,347 cm^3, and Blacks averaged 1,267 cm^3. Naturally the averages vary between samples and the races do overlap. But the results from different methods on different samples show the same average pattern — Orientals > Whites > Blacks.

Conclusion

Studies of race differences in brain size use a number of methods, including MRI. All methods produce the same results. Orientals have the largest brains (on average), Blacks the smallest, and Whites in between. These differences in brain size are not due to body size. Adjusting for body size still results in the same pattern. The three-way pattern is also true for IQ. These race differences in brain size mean that Orientals average about 102 million more brain cells than Whites, and that Whites have about 480 million more than Blacks. These differences in brain size probably explain the racial differences in IQ and cultural achievement.

Additional Readings

Jensen, A. R. (1998). *The g Factor*. Westport, CT: Praeger.

Rushton, J. P. & Ankney, C. D. (1996). Brain size and cognitive ability: Correlations with age, sex, social class, and race. *Psychonomic Bulletin and Review, 3,* 21-36.

5

Genes, Environment, or Both?

A number of studies show that race differences are caused by both genes and environment. Heritabilities, cross-race adoptions, genetic weights, and regression-to-the-average all tell the same story. Cross-race adoptions give some of the best proof that the genes cause race differences in IQ. Growing up in a middle-class White home does not lower the average IQ for Orientals nor raise it for Blacks.

Can any environmental factor explain all the data on speed of dental development, age of sexual maturity, brain size, IQ, testosterone level, and the number of multiple births? Genes seem to be involved. But how can we know for sure?

Some traits are clearly inherited. For example, we know that the race differences in twinning rate are due to heredity and not to the environment. Studies of Oriental, White, and Mixed-Race children in Hawaii and of White, Black, and Mixed-Race children in Brazil show that it is the mother's race, and not the father's, that is the determining factor. But the role of racial heredity is found for other traits as well.

Heritability Studies

Heritability is the amount of variation in a trait due to the genes. A heritability of 1.00 means that the differences are inborn and the environment has no effect. A heritability of zero (0.00) means the trait is controlled by the environment and not at all by the genes. A heritability of 0.50 means that the differences come from both the genes and the environment.

Heritability is useful for animal breeders. They like to know how much genes influence things like milk yields and beefiness in cattle or determine which dogs can hunt, and which are good with children. The higher the heritability, the more the offspring will resemble their parents. On the other hand, low heritabilities mean that environmental factors like diet and health are more important.

For people, we measure heritability by comparing family members, especially identical with fraternal twins, and adopted children with ordinary brothers and sisters. Identical twins share 100% of their genes, while fraternal twins share only 50%. Ordinary brothers and sisters also share 50% of their genes, while adopted children share no genes. If genes are important, identical twins should be twice as similar to each other as are fraternal twins or ordinary siblings — and so they are.

Some identical twins are separated early in life and grow up apart. The famous Minnesota Twin Study by

Thomas J. Bouchard and others compared many of these. (See Chart 8).

Even though they grew up in different homes, identical twins grow to be very similar to each other. They are similar both in physical traits (like height and fingerprints) and in behavioral traits (like IQ and personality).

Identical twins who grow up in different homes share all their genes but do not share the effects of upbringing. As you can see in Chart 8, heredity accounted for 97% of the difference for fingerprints, and the environment only 3%. Social attitudes were 40% heredity, 60% environment. IQ was 70% heredity, 30% environment.

Identical twins are often so alike that even close friends cannot tell them apart. Although the twins in the Minnesota Project lived separate lives, they shared many likes and dislikes. They often had the same hobbies and enjoyed the same music, food, and clothes. Their manners and gestures were often the same. The twins were very alike in when they got married (and sometimes divorced) and in the jobs they held. They even gave similar names to their children and pets.

One of these pairs, the "Jim twins," were adopted as infants by two different working- class families. But they marked their lives with a trail of similar names. Both named their childhood pet "Toy". Both married and divorced women named Linda and then married women named Betty. One twin named his son James Allen, the other named his son James Alan.

Chart 8

Similarity in Identical Twins Reared Apart

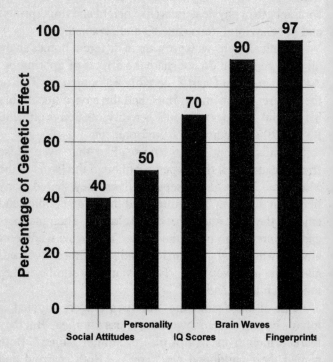

Source: Third Unabridged Edition of *Race, Evolution, and Behavior* (pp. 45-47).

Another pair of separated twins were helpless gigglers. Each twin said her adoptive parents were reserved and serious. Each one said she never met anyone who laughed as easily as she did -- until she met her twin!

Heredity also affects the sex drive. The age of our first sexual experience, how often we have sex, and our total number of sexual partners all have heritabilities of about 50%. So do the odds that we will get divorced. Several studies find that homosexuality, lesbianism, and other sexual orientations are about 50% genetic.

Twin studies show that even social attitudes are partly genetic in origin. One Australian study of 4,000 twin pairs found there was a genetic influence on specific political beliefs like capital punishment, abortion, and immigration.

It turns out that criminal tendency is also heritable. About 50% of identical twins with criminal records have twins with criminal records, while only about 25% of fraternal twins do.

Genes influence helping behavior and aggression. A large study of British twins found that the desire to help or hurt others has a heritability of around 50%. For men, fighting, carrying a weapon, and struggling with a police officer are all about 50% heritable.

My article in the 1989 *Behavioral and Brain Sciences* shows that who we marry and who we choose as friends is also partly genetic. When the blood groups and heritabilities of friends and spouses are compared, we find that people chose partners who are genetically similar to themselves. The tendency for like to attract like is rooted in the genes.

Adoption Studies

A good check on the results of twin studies comes from adoption studies. A Danish study (in the 1984 issue of *Science*) examined 14,427 children separated from their birth parents as infants. Boys were more likely to have a criminal record if their birth parents had a criminal record than if their adoptive parents did. Even though they were brought up in different homes, 20% of the full brothers and 13% of the half-brothers had similar criminal records. Only 9% of the unrelated boys brought up in the same home both had criminal records.

The Colorado Adoption Project found that genes increase in influence as we age. Between age 3 and 16, adopted children grew to be more like their birth parents in height, weight, and IQ. By age 16 the adopted children did not resemble the people who had reared them. The heritability of height, weight, and IQ in infancy are all about 30%. By the teenage years, they are about 50%, and by adulthood, they are about 80%. Thus, as children grow older, their home environments have less impact and their genes have more impact, just the opposite of what culture theory predicts.

Race and Heritability

Can heritability tell us anything about the differences *between* races? Yes, a lot! Studies show that when the heritability is high in Whites, it is also high in Orientals and Blacks. When it is low in Whites, it is also low in Orientals and Blacks. For example, the heritability of IQ is about 50% for Blacks, Orientals, and other groups, just as it is for Whites. So there is a genetic basis for intelligence in all three races.

One study used the Armed Services Vocational Aptitude Battery (ASVAB), given to many men and women going into the military. It found that in all three races the similarity among siblings was the same. The genetic influence on IQ in Orientals, Whites, and Blacks is about equal. There is no special factor, like the history of slavery or White racism, that has made cultural influences stronger for one race than for another.

Trans-racial Adoption Studies

The best evidence for the genetic basis of race-IQ differences comes from trans-racial adoption studies of Oriental children, Black children, and Mixed-Race children. All these children have been adopted by White parents at an early age and have grown up in middle-class White homes.

One well known trans-racial adoption study is Sandra Scarr's Minnesota project. The adopted children were either White, Black, or Mixed-Race (Black-White) babies. The children took IQ tests when they were seven years old and again when they were 17.

In their initial report, the authors thought that their study proved that a good home could raise the IQs of Black children. At age 7, their IQ was 97, well above the Black average of 85 and almost equal to the White average of 100. However, when the children were retested at age

17, the results told another story (reported in the 1992 issue of *Intelligence*).

At age seven, Black, Mixed-Race, and White adopted children all had higher IQ scores than average for their group. Growing up in a good home helped all the children. Even so, the racial pattern was exactly as predicted by genetic theory, not by culture theory. Black children reared in these good homes had an average IQ of 97, but the Mixed-Race children averaged an IQ of 109, and the White children an IQ of 112.

The evidence for genetic theory got stronger as the children grew older. By age 17, the IQs of the adopted children moved closer to the expected average for their race. At age 17 adopted White children had an IQ of about 106, Mixed-Race adoptees an IQ of about 99, and adopted Blacks had an IQ of about 89. IQ scores are not the only evidence in this study. School grades, class ranks, and aptitude tests show the same pattern.

When Sandra Scarr got the results of her follow-up study at age 17, she changed her mind about the cause of why the Blacks and Whites differed. She wrote, "those adoptees with two African American birth parents had IQs that were not notably higher than the IQ scores of Black youngsters reared in Black families." Growing up in a White middle-class home produced little or no lasting increase in the IQs of Black children.

Some psychologists disagreed with her. They claimed "expectancy effects," not genes, explained the pattern. They argued that the Black and White children were not treated the same. Even if parents took good care of their children, the schools, classmates, and society as a whole discriminated against Black children and this hurt their IQs. Because we *expected* Black children to do poorly in school, they lived up to our low expectations.

Is there any way to decide between the genetic theory and the expectancy theory? There is. A special analysis of the Scarr study compared parents who believed that they had adopted a Black baby but, really, had adopted a Mixed-Race (Black-White) child. The average IQ for these Mixed-Race children was just about the same as for other Mixed-Race children and above that for adopted Black children. This was true even though the parents who adopted these Mixed-Race children thought their babies really had two Black parents.

Chart 9 summarizes the results for Oriental children adopted into White middle-class homes. Korean and Vietnamese babies from poor backgrounds, many of whom were malnourished, were adopted by White American and Belgian families. When they grew up, they excelled in school. The IQs of the adopted Oriental children were 10 or more points higher than the national average for the country they grew up in. Trans-racial adoption does not increase or decrease IQ. The three-way pattern of race differences in IQ remains.

The Minnesota Transracial Adoption Study also showed that there are race differences in personality. Black 17-year-olds were more active and more disruptive than White 17-year-olds. Korean children raised in White American families were quieter and less active than White children.

Chart 9

IQ Scores for Adopted Children of Various Races After Being Reared in White Middle-Class Homes (Average of Scores at Ages 7 and 17)

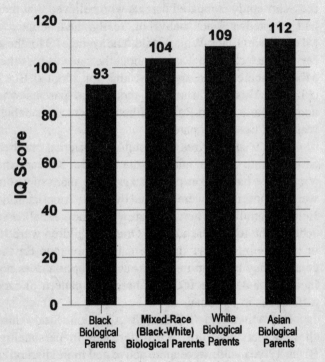

Source: Third Unabridged Edition of *Race, Evolution, and Behavior* (pp. 187-194)

Heritabilities Predict Racial Differences

There are other ways to test the influence of genes and environment on race differences in IQ. Some test items have higher heritability, i.e. they are more the result of heredity than others. If genes cause the Black-White IQ differences, then Blacks and Whites should differ on these high heritability items. Arthur Jensen's 1998 book, *The g Factor*, shows that indeed race difference are higher on tests with higher heritability, even for toddlers.

Inbreeding depression gives us still another way to test if genes explain Black-White differences. It occurs when harmful recessive genes combine and lowers height, health, and IQ. Inbreeding depression is more likely when children are born to closely related people (such as cousins). Most IQ tests are made up of several sub-tests such as vocabulary, memory, and logical reasoning.

The children of cousin marriages have a lower IQ than do other children and their scores are more depressed on some IQ sub-tests than on others. The more inbreeding depression affects a sub-test, the more we know that genes affect sub-test performance. Therefore, genetic theory predicts that the tests showing the most inbreeding depression will also show the most Black-White difference.

In a study published in *Intelligence* in 1989 I looked at the amount of inbreeding depression on scores among cousin marriages in Japan for 11 sub-tests of a well known IQ test. Then I compared which sub-tests showed the most inbreeding depression and which ones had the most Black-White difference in the U.S. The sub-tests that showed the most inbreeding depression also showed the most Black-White differences. Since the inbreeding depression numbers came from a study of Japanese cousin marriages, the cultural differences between Blacks and Whites in the U.S. cannot explain why Blacks find some IQ sub-tests harder than others.

Regression to the Average

Regression to the Average provides still another way to test if race differences are genetic. The children of very tall parents are taller than average. But they are shorter than their parents and nearer the average of their race. Similarly, children of very short parents are shorter than average, but taller than their parents. This is called the Law of Regression to the Average. It is not true just for height, but for IQ as well. Most physical and psychological traits show some regression effect.

Regression to the Average happens when very tall (or very high IQ) people mate because they pass on some, but not all, of their exceptional genes to their offspring. The same thing happens with very short (or very low IQ) people. It's like rolling a pair of dice and having them come up two sixes or two ones. The odds are that on the next roll, you'll get some value that is not as high (or as low).

Here's why regression is important to our studies. Because Whites and Blacks come from different races, they have many different genes. The Law of Regression predicts that for any trait, scores will return to the average of their race. The Regression Law predicts that in the U.S.,

Black children with parents of IQ 115 will regress toward the Black average of 85, while White children with parents of IQ 115 will regress only toward the White average of 100.

The law also works at the other end of the scale. Black children with parents of IQ 70 will move up toward the Black average IQ of 85, but White children with parents of IQ 70 will move further up toward the White average of 100. When we test these predictions about Regression to the Average from parent to child they prove true.

The Regression Law also works for brothers and sisters. Black and White children matched for IQs of 120 have siblings who show different amounts of regression. Black siblings regress toward an IQ of 85, while White siblings regress only to 100. The opposite happens at the lower end of the scale. Black and White children matched for IQs of 70 have siblings who regress differently. Black siblings regress toward an average of 85, whereas White siblings move to 100.

Regression to the Average explains another interesting finding. Black children born to rich parents have IQs that are two to four points lower than do White children born to poor parents. The high IQ Black parents were not able to pass on their IQ advantage to their children even though they did give them good nutrition, good medical care, and good schools. Only genes plus environment tell the whole story.

Conclusion

Genes play a big part in IQ, personality, attitudes, and other behaviors. This is true for Orientals, Whites, and Blacks. Trans-racial adoption studies (where infants of one race are adopted and reared by parents of a different race), studies of regression to the mean (which compare parents and siblings in the different racial groups), and of inbreeding depression (which study the children of closely-related parents) all provide evidence for why genes cause the races to differ in IQ and personality. No purely cultural theory can explain these results, which are not only explained but *predicted* by genetic theory.

Additional Readings

Jensen, A. R. (1998). *The g Factor*. Westport, CT: Praeger.

Weinberg, R. A., Scarr, S., & Waldman, I. D. (1992). The Minnesota Transracial Adoption Study: A follow-up of IQ test performance at adolescence. *Intelligence, 16,* 117-135.

6

Life History Theory

The theory of r-K life histories explains the worldwide three-way pattern in race differences. The r-strategy means being very sexually active and having many offspring. The K-strategy means having fewer offspring, but with both mother and father giving them more care. Humans are the most K strategists of all species. Among humans, Orientals follow the most K-strategy, Blacks the most r-strategy, and Whites fall in between.

The previous chapters showed that there are important race differences in brain size, hormone levels, even bone and tooth development, as well as sexual behavior, aggression, and crime. The three-way pattern in which the races differ -- Orientals at one end, Blacks at the other, and Whites in between -- is true all around the world. A look at history shows that the race differences we see today were also seen in the past.

Why do the races differ? Of course, poverty, nutrition, and cultural factors are important. But so too are the genes. Culture theory alone cannot explain all the findings.

r-K Life History Theory

Harvard University biologist E.O. Wilson was the first to use the term r-K Life-History Theory. He used it to explain population change in plants and animals. I have applied it to the human races.

A life-history is a genetically-organized group of traits that have evolved together to meet the trials of life -- survival, growth, and reproduction. For our purposes, r is a term in Wilson's equation that stands for the natural rate of reproduction (the number of offspring). The symbol K stands for the amount of care parents give to insure that their offspring survive. Plants and animals have different life history strategies. Some are more r and others are relatively more K.

The r and K strategists differ in the number of eggs they produce. The r-strategists are like machine-gunners. They fire so many shots that at least one of them will hit the target. The r-strategists produce many eggs and sperm, and mate and give birth often. The K-strategists, on the other hand, are like snipers. They put time and effort into a few carefully placed shots. K-strategists give their offspring a lot of care. They work together in getting food and shelter, help their kin, and have complex social systems.   That is why the K-strategists need a more complex nervous system and bigger brain, but produce fewer eggs and sperm.

This basic law of evolution links reproductive strategy to intelligence and brain development. The less complex an animal's brain, the greater its reproductive output. The bigger an animal's brain, the longer it takes to reach sexual maturity and the fewer offspring it produces (see Chart 10). Oysters, for example, have a nervous system so simple that they lack a true brain. To offset this they produce 500 million eggs a year. In contrast, chimpanzees have large brains but give birth to one baby about every four years.

In different species of plants and animals we find a consistent pattern between these two variables -- intelligence and reproductive rate. The number of offspring, the time between births, the amount of care parents give, infant mortality, speed of maturity, life span, even social organization, altruism, and brain size all fit together like pieces of a puzzle. The complete puzzle forms a picture biologists call the r-K Life History Strategy.

The r-type life history involves higher levels of reproduction, while the K-type strategy requires greater parental care and use of mental attributes. Since larger brains need more time to be built, all the stages of development are also slowed down.

The gestation period for some smaller-brained primates (like lemurs and monkeys) is 18 weeks. But for bigger-brained primates (like chimpanzees and gorillas) it is 33 weeks. Some monkeys have their first pregnancy at the age of nine *months*. Gorillas, which have bigger brains and greater intelligence, have their first pregnancy at ten *years*.

Chart 10

The r-K Scale of Reproductive Strategy: Balancing Egg Output versus Parental Care

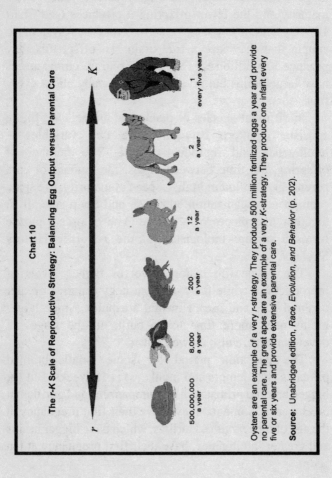

| 500,000,000 a year | 8,000 a year | 200 a year | 12 a year | 2 a year | 1 every five years |

Oysters are an example of a very r-strategy. They produce 500 million fertilized eggs a year and provide no parental care. The great apes are an example of a very K-strategy. They produce one infant every five or six years and provide extensive parental care.

Source: Unabridged edition, *Race, Evolution, and Behavior* (p. 202).

Chart 11

Some Life-History Differences Between
r-Strategists and *K*-Strategists

r-strategist	*K*-strategist
Family characteristics	
Large litter size	Small litter size
Short birth spacing	Long birth spacing
Many offspring	Few offspring
High infant mortality	Low infant mortality
Little parental care	Much parental care
Individual characteristics	
Rapid maturation	Slow maturation
Early sexual reproduction	Delayed sexual reproduction
Short life	Long life
High reproductive effort	Low reproductive effort
High energy utilization	Efficient energy utilization
Smaller brains	Larger brains
Population characteristics	
Opportunistic exploiters	Consistent exploiters
Dispersing colonizers	Stable occupiers
Variable population size	Stable population size
Weak competition	Strong competition
Social system characteristics	
Low social organization	High social organization
Low altruism	High altruism

Source: Unabridged edition, *Race, Evolution, and Behavior* (p. 203).

Chart 12

Increasing Gestation Times, Life Spans, and Life Phases in Primates

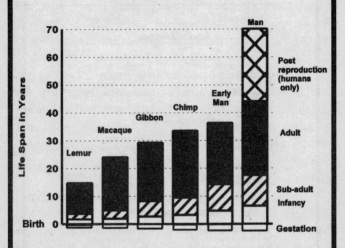

Most *r* ⟵⟶ Most *K*

Each step in the *r - K* scale puts more energy into child care and increased survival of offspring.

Source: Unabridged edition, *Race, Evolution, and Behavior* (p. 205).

Monkeys are born with a brain very nearly 100% its adult size, while chimpanzees and gorillas are born with about 60% of adult brain size. Human babies are born with a brain that is less than 30% of its adult size. For the first few months of life, monkeys are better than apes in most tests of sensory-motor behavior. And infant apes are superior to infant humans on these tasks. The r-K relationship is true for different species and also applies to humans.

Chart 10 shows where various animals fall on the r-K scale. Different species are, of course, only relatively r or K. Rabbits are K-strategists compared to fish. But they are r-strategists compared to primates (monkeys, apes, and humans, who are the best K-strategists among mammals). Humans may be the most K species of all. And some humans are better K-strategists than others.

Chart 11 lists traits typical of r and K reproductive strategies. Every species and every race has a certain life history that we can describe in terms of r-K. The position of each species (or race) on the r-K scale shows the strategy that gave its ancestors the best chance to survive in their habitat.

Chart 12 shows the life phases and gestation times (conception to birth) for six different primates. They show a scale of increasing K, from lemur to macaque, to gibbon, to chimp, to early humans, to modern humans. Each step in the scale means that the species puts more time and energy into caring for its young and insuring their survival. Each step also means not having as many offspring. Note the different sizes of each of the phases for the different species in Chart 12. Only humans have the postreproductive (i.e., after menopause) phase.

The differences in *r-K* strategies that exist even in primates are important. A female lemur is an *r*-strategist for a primate. She produces her first offspring at nine months and has a life expectancy of only 15 years. A female gorilla is a *K*-strategist. She has her first pregnancy at about age 10 years and can expect to live to the age of 40. The lemur may mature, have a number of young, and die before the gorilla has her first baby.

Race Differences and *r-K* Strategies

How do the three races fall along the *r-K* scale? Look back at the pattern of racial differences in Chart 1 (page 19). Compare them to the *r-K* traits in Chart 11 (page 77). Orientals are the most *K*, Blacks are the most *r*, and Whites fall in between. Being more *r* means:

- shorter gestation periods
- earlier physical maturation (muscular control, bone and dental development)
- smaller brains
- earlier puberty (age at first menstruation, first intercourse, first pregnancy)
- more developed primary sexual characteristics (size of penis, vagina, testes, ovaries)
- more developed secondary sexual characteristics (voice, muscularity, buttocks, breasts)
- more biological than social control of behavior (length of menstrual cycle, periodicity of sexual response, predictability of life history from start of puberty)

- higher levels of sex hormones (testosterone, gonadotropins, follicle stimulating hormone)
- higher levels of individuality (lower law abidingness)
- more permissive sexual attitudes
- higher intercourse frequencies (premarital, marital, extramarital)
- weaker pair bonds
- more siblings
- higher rates of child neglect and abandonment
- greater frequency of disease
- shorter life expectancy

Testosterone -- The Master Switch?

Testosterone may be a master switch that sets the position of the races on the r-K scale. We know that this male sex hormone affects self-concept, temperament, sexuality, aggression and altruism. It controls the development of muscles and the deepening of the voice. It can also contribute to aggression and problem behavior. A study of over 4,000 military veterans found high testosterone levels predicted greater criminality, alcohol and drug abuse, military misconduct, and having many sex partners.

We can now see how different testosterone levels among the three races might explain the r-K behavioral differences. With higher testosterone levels, Blacks are more likely to put time and energy into having offspring. On the other hand, Asians and Whites with lower testosterone levels put more time and energy into caring for a few offspring and making long term plans. But, how did this happen? And why? For the answers we must turn to human origins and the Out-of-Africa theory of racial evolution.

Conclusion

r-K Life History Theory, a basic principle of modern evolutionary biology, explains the three-way pattern of differences in brain size, IQ, and behavior, described earlier. Every species of plant or animal can be placed on the *r-K* scale. The *r* end of the scale means having more offspring, maturing earlier, having smaller brains and providing less parental care. The *K* end of the scale means having fewer offspring, maturing later, having larger brains, and providing more parental care. Humans are the most *K* species of all. Among humans, Orientals are the most *K*, Blacks the most *r*, and Whites fall in between.

Additional Readings

Johanson, D. C. & Edey, M. A. (1981). *Lucy: The Beginnings of Humankind*. New York: Simon & Schuster.

Lovejoy, C.O. (1981). The origin of man. *Science, 211*, 341-350.

7

Out of Africa

The latest theory of human origins -- Out-of-Africa -- provides the final piece to the puzzle. It explains why r-K theory accounts for race differences in body, brain, and behavior. As races moved out of Africa they evolved away from r-type behaviors and toward K-type. Moving out of Africa meant increasing brain size and IQ, but lowering reproduction, aggression and sexual activity.

Based on his theory of evolution, Charles Darwin thought Africa was "the cradle of mankind." He did not have any fossils from Africa to support his theory but he concluded that humans came from Africa based on watching the chimpanzee and the gorilla. If the African apes were our closest living relatives, it made sense that humans first evolved on the only continent where all three species lived.

Evidence from genetics, the fossil record, and archaeology have since all proved Darwin correct. The human line began with the African fossil species called

Australopithecus. Later human ancestors *Homo erectus* and then *Homo sapiens* also appeared first in Africa.

Homo sapiens were fully human. They were in Africa less than 200,000 years ago. Moving to the Middle East about 100,000 years ago, they then spread out across the world. They replaced the Neanderthal and *Homo erectus* groups they met either by fighting or competing for food.

When modern humans left Africa they began to develop the racial traits we see today by adapting to the new regions and climates. The first split in the human line took place about 100,000 years ago between groups that remained in Africa (ancestors to modern Blacks) and those who left Africa. Then about 40,000 years ago the group that left Africa divided once again, into the ancestors of today's Whites and Orientals.

This history of moving first out of Africa into Europe and then later into East Asia explains why Whites fall in between Orientals and Blacks on the life history variables. The split between Africans and non-Africans happened first, almost twice as early as the split between Orientals and Whites.

The Out of Africa theory explains the good fit between the r-K life history traits and race differences. It is hard to survive in Africa. Africa has unpredictable droughts and deadly diseases that spread quickly. More Africans than Asians or Europeans die young -- often from tropical disease. In these African conditions, parental care is a less certain way of making sure a child will survive. A better strategy is simply to have more children. This tilts their life history toward the r-end of the r-K scale. A more r-strategy means not only more offspring and less parental care. It also means less culture is passed from parent to child, and this tends to reduce the intellectual demands needed to function in the culture. And the process continues from one generation to the next.

In contrast, the humans migrating to Eurasia faced entirely new problems -- gathering and storing food, providing shelter, making clothes, and raising children during the long winters. These tasks were more mentally demanding. They called for larger brains and slower growth rates. They permitted lower levels of sex hormones, resulting in less sexual potency and aggression and more family stability and longevity. Leaving the tropics for the northern continents meant leaving the r-strategy for the K-strategy -- and all that went with it.

The Evidence

How can we know if the Out of Africa theory is true? To answer that question, we have to look at the evidence from genetics, paleontology, and archaeology.

The History and Geography of Human Genes (1994) by Luigi Cavalli-Sforza and his colleagues looks at thousands of genetic DNA comparisons of the races. Geneticists count the number of gene mutations in each group to measure which groups are most closely related and when the groups split from one another. These DNA studies support the Out of Africa theory that the split between Africans and all other groups was the first to take place.

Fossils of prehistoric humans tell us that early steps in our evolution took place in Africa. *Homo sapiens* lived in

Africa between 200,000 and 100,000 years ago, but they only reached the Middle East about 100,000 years ago. Earlier hominids such as the Neanderthals were very different from modern humans. They had faces that jut further forward and they had larger front teeth than any living Europeans, Africans, or East Asians. Neanderthals had denser bones, thicker skulls, and more pronounced brow ridges than any modern humans. By comparison, all living humans are alike, despite our race differences.

Archaeology tells us the same story. The crude, Early Stone Age culture (termed Lower Paleolithic) of *Homo erectus*, existed more than one million years before *Homo sapiens* appeared. The Early Stone Age tool kit had hand-axes, choppers, and cleavers, all very similar in shape. However, the Middle Stone Age tool kit of the Neanderthals (termed Middle Paleolithic) included more advanced stone tools and the use of bone.

When modern humans first appeared on the scene 100,000 years ago, things started to change in major ways. The Late Stone Age tool kit (termed Upper Paleolithic) was highly specialized. It consisted of thinner blades struck off of stone cores to make knives, spear barbs, scrapers and cutters. Standardized bone and antler tools appeared in the tool kit for the first time, including needles for sewing fur clothes. The Late Stone Age tool kit contained tools made of several parts tied or glued together. Spear points were set in shafts and ax heads in handles. Rope was used to make nets to trap foxes, rabbits, and other small animals. Advanced weapons like barbed harpoons, darts, spear-throwers, and bows and arrows gave

Late Stone Age people the ability to kill animals from a safe distance.

Survival in Northeast Asia about 40,000 years ago also required warm clothing. Archeologists have found needles, cave paintings of parkas, and grave ornaments marking the outlines of shirts and trousers. We know that warm furs were worn. Fox and wolf skeletons missing their paws tell us that these animals were skinned to make fur clothes. Houses were dug into the ground to provide insulation. These large dwellings were marked by post holes and had walls made from mammoth bones. Fireplaces and stone lamps were used to light the long Arctic winter night.

Geography and Race

Africa is warmer than the northern continents, but it is a less stable habitat. Droughts, storms, and diseases from viruses, bacteria, and parasites cause high death rates, even today. Without modern medical care, insuring survival in Africa means having many young (*r*-strategy). In the more stable environments of Europe and Asia, survival is insured from having fewer young, but caring for them very well (*K*-strategy).

The environment of Eurasia produced physical differences between the races. Northern Europe's cloudiness meant less sunshine. This decreased the intake of vitamin D, so lighter skin and hair were needed to let more sunlight get in. As a result, Europeans born with lighter skin and hair were healthier. They had more chance of having children who would survive and reproduce.

East Asia was even colder than North Europe, but with less cloud cover and more sunlight. There a thicker layer of fat helped to insulate against the cold. This gives many Orientals a so-called "yellow" complexion because it reduces the visibility of red blood vessels close to the skin. Meanwhile in Africa melanin gives the skin a black color to protect it from the scorching rays of the sun.

Climate differences also influenced mental abilities. In Africa, food and warmth were available all year round. To survive the cold winters, the populations migrating northwards had to become more inventive. They had to find new sources of food and methods for storing it. They needed to make clothing and shelters to protect against the elements. Without them the people would have died. Both parents had to provide more care to help their young survive in the harsher climates.

Whites and Orientals in Eurasia had to find food and keep warm in the colder climates. In the tropics, plant foods were plentiful all year round. In Europe and Asia they were seasonal and could not be found during many winter and spring months.

To survive the long winters, the ancestors of today's Whites and Orientals made complex tools and weapons to fish and hunt animals. They made spearheads that could kill big game from a greater distance and knives for cutting and skinning. Fires, clothes and shelters were made for warmth. Bone needles were used to sew animal skins together and shelters were made from large bones and skins.

Making special tools, fires, clothing and shelters called for higher intelligence. Moving "Out of Africa" meant moving into a K-type life-history strategy. That meant higher IQ, larger brains, slower growth, and lower hormone levels. It also meant lower levels of sexuality, aggression, and impulsive behavior. More family stability, advanced planning, self-control, rule-following, and longevity were needed.

Conclusion

Fossil records, archaeology, and genetic DNA studies of the living races support Charles Darwin's insight that we evolved in Africa. Humans then spread to the Middle East, Europe, Asia, Australia, and then to the Americas. As humans left Africa, their bodies, brains and behavior changed. To deal with the colder winters and scarcer food supply of Europe and Northeast Asia, the Oriental and White races moved away from an r-strategy toward the K-strategy. This meant more parenting and social organization, which required a larger brain size and a higher IQ.

Additional Readings

Cavalli-Sforza, L. L., Menozzi, P., & Piazza, A. (1994). *The History and Geography of Human Genes*. Princeton, NJ: Princeton.University Press.
Stringer, C. & McKie, R. (1996). *African Exodus*. London: Cape.

8

Questions and Answers

*This final chapter lists the most important
questions I have been asked about my r-K
theory and my answers to them. It also
gives pointers to the earlier chapter(s)
that discuss each topic in greater
detail, my closing thoughts on* Race,
Evolution, and Behavior, *and on
the story of the abridged edition.*

You may be asking, "Why is the information about
race in this book so different from what I have seen in
magazines, college texts, and on TV?" The answer is that
about 70 years ago the social sciences took a wrong turn.
They left Darwinism and refused to look at the biological
basis of human behavior -- evolution and genetics. They
also divided into separate academic fields and lost the
forest for the trees.

In this book I try to re-unite the social and biological
sciences on the issue of race. The evidence I have used
comes from the best scientific journals, not from obscure
sources. I began to study and publish scientific articles on
race in the early 1980s. Since then I have received many

questions about my work. Probably you've thought of some of these questions yourself.

This final chapter lists the questions I have been asked most often and my answers to them. I've grouped the questions by major topic. Each topic has a pointer to the chapter(s) in this abridged edition that discuss the topic in detail.

Is Race a Useful Concept? (Chapter 1)

Q: You write as if race is a valid biological concept. Aren't you only repeating the stereotypes of 18th and 19th century Europeans?

A: True, there is a 200-year history of "European" research on race. But similar descriptions were made by Arab and Turkish writers nearly 1,000 years earlier and some can even be traced back to the ancient Greeks. Today, new methods of genetic DNA analysis agree with the original classifications made by early European scientists based on their observations.

Q: But isn't race "just skin deep"? Don't most scientists now agree that race is a social construct, not a biological reality?

A: Biological evidence shows that race is not a social construct. Coroners in crime labs can identify race from a skeleton or even just the skull. They can identify race from blood, hair, or semen as well. To deny the existence of race is unscientific and unrealistic. Race is much more than "just skin deep."

Q: Your three major racial categories overlap and it isn't possible to assign each person to a race. So isn't your three-way racial classification scheme somewhat made-up?

A: Yes, to a certain extent all the races blend into each other. That is true in any biological classification system. However, most people can be clearly identified with one race or another. In both everyday life and evolutionary biology, a "Black" is anyone most of whose ancestors were born in sub-Saharan Africa. A "White" is anyone most of whose ancestors were born in Europe. And an "Oriental" is anyone most of whose ancestors were born in East Asia. Modern DNA studies give pretty much the same results.

Q: Doesn't the Out of Africa theory imply that we are "all Africans under the skin"?

A: Yes and no. The theory is that *Homo sapiens* first appeared in Africa about 200,000 years ago. Then some groups migrated north about 110,000 years ago into Europe and Asia. A further split took place between the "ancestral Whites" and the "ancestral Orientals" about 40,000 years ago. True all humans are brothers (and sisters). But we all know that brothers and sisters can still be very different from one another.

Q: All Whites aren't the same. All Blacks aren't alike. Neither are all Orientals. Isn't there more variation within races than between them?

A: There is a lot of variation within each of the three races. The full range of variation will be found within any of the major racial groups. Still, group averages are important. Each racial group has a bell curve distribution with some people at the high end and some at the low end, and most people in the middle.

Groups with a high average will have many more people at the high end and not so many people at the low end. The 6-point IQ difference between Orientals and Whites and the 15-point IQ difference between Whites and Blacks means that a higher percentage of Orientals and a lower percentage of Blacks end up in the highest IQ categories. Those percentages have real implications in school and at work.

The same is true for crime. Most people of any race are hard-working and law abiding. There is no "criminal race." However, the difference in average crime rate means that a much higher percentage of Blacks can fall into a life of crime. The 85 average IQ of criminals is almost identical with the 85 average IQ of Blacks, so IQ is related to crime. Although Blacks make up only about 12% of the U.S. population, each year they commit about half of all crimes.

Q: Why do you base so much of your argument on the differences between the three major races? Are you not ignoring divisions and sub-groups within the three races?

A: Of course there are subdivisions within the three major races. The Oriental group can be subdivided into Northeast Asians (such as the Chinese, Japanese, and Koreans) and the Southeast Asians (such as the Filipinos and Malays). Black and White groups can also be subdivided in the same way. Nevertheless, my simplified three-way division serves a purpose. In science, a concept is useful if it groups facts so that general laws and conclusions can be drawn from them. The three-way classification is scientifically justified because it shows a consistent pattern for many different traits, with Orientals at one end, Blacks at the other, and Whites in between.

Are the Race Differences Real?
(Chapters 2 through 5)

Q: Haven't you just chosen the studies that fit with your three-way race pattern and ignored all the ones that do not?

A: If that were true, where are the studies I have ignored? I have not ignored any important studies. Whenever averages are used from several studies, the same three-way pattern of race differences appears.

Q: Aren't some of the studies you use, especially those on race and brain size, very old? Haven't they been shown to be examples of racist bias rather than honest reports of scientific facts?

A: No. Even the most recent studies, using the latest technology (such as Magnetic Resonance Imaging to measure brain size), give the same results as the older studies. These state-of-the-art studies of brain size are reviewed in Chapter 4. They are much more precise studies than the older ones, but produce almost exactly the same results. Only "political correctness" caused the early findings to "vanish" from the scientific radar screen. If there is any bias, it is on the part of those who choose to misrepresent both the older studies and the recent research on race and brain size to justify a social agenda they want to promote.

Q: Aren't you really producing the race differences by averaging the results of many studies? Wouldn't it be better just to look at the very best studies?

A: Using an average of all the data is better than using any single measurement or study. When you take an average, the errors fade and real differences appear. Hundreds of studies published in the best journals show the three-way pattern of race differences.

Q: Isn't it possible to get a pattern of race differences in brain size (or IQ or any trait) simply by using the studies that support the point you are trying to make?

A: That's exactly why it is better to average all the data. Averages are used for many sports competitions including some Olympic events, public opinion polls about upcoming elections, or the stock market performance with the Dow Jones Average. The same is true when studying race, brain size, IQ, and crime.

Is the Relationship Between Race and Crime Valid? (Chapter 2)

Q: Your three-way pattern in race differences in crime is based on official reports of arrests and convictions. But don't self-report studies show that there are no race differences in crime?

A: Self-reports show a smaller race difference than the official arrest and conviction records. However, self-reports are only valid as a measure of less violent crime. They often include minor items like "Have you ever been in a fight?" or "Would you worry about being in debt?" Unlike official crime reports, they often give no facts about the frequency of criminal behavior. Self-reports do not distinguish between career criminals and first offenders.

Q: But don't the arrest and conviction statistics from U.S. police departments and the FBI reflect America's history of racism?

A: INTERPOL Yearbooks show the same three-way pattern of race differences in crime. African and Caribbean countries have twice as many violent crimes per person as do European countries and three times as many as do the Asian Pacific Rim countries like Japan and China.

Q: Aren't Black Americans really the victims of crime, not the cause?

A: Many Blacks are indeed victims of crime. And there are many White and Oriental criminals. Nevertheless, the criminals are disproportionately Black. U. S. Department of Justice statistics report that Blacks are 60 times more likely to attack Whites than Whites are to attack Blacks. For the 20% of violent crimes that are interracial, 15% involve Black offenders and White victims; 2% involve White offenders and Black victims.

Is the Relationship Between Race and Reproduction Valid? (Chapter 3)

Q: Doesn't the evidence on race and penis size come from 19th Century stories by racist Europeans in colonial Africa?

A: The earliest findings come from the Arabic explorers in Africa and one study by a French army surgeon originally published in 1898. More up-to-date information comes from the World Health Organization. Their studies show the same three-way race pattern as do all the other studies.

Q: Isn't the material on race and sex a kind of pornography? Isn't race controversial enough without bringing sex and AIDS into the picture?

A: One World Health Organization study I mentioned in the previous answer examined penis size in order to provide the right size condoms to slow the spread of AIDS. Finding out which groups are most at risk for sexually transmitted diseases can help slow their spread and save lives.

Is the Genetic Evidence Flawed? (Chapter 5)

Q: How can you talk about a genetic basis for intelligence, criminality, or sexuality? No one has ever found a gene responsible for any of these. Brain size and structure may be genetic, but we still do not know exactly which genes are important for IQ or how they work.

A: New research is providing the answer. Every day the newspaper or TV reports that someone has just found a gene for alcoholism, intelligence, impulsivity, aggression, longevity, or other human behavior. When the Human Genome Project has finished mapping all our genes, we will know even more about the genetic basis of behavior.

Q: Isn't this Genetic Determinism?

A: I never claimed that race differences are 100% genetic. Obviously, environmental factors are important. The scientific argument is really between "hereditarians" and "egalitarians." Hereditarians, like myself, think the best explanation of why the races differ involves both genes and environment. Egalitarians claim the races differ for 100% cultural reasons and some of them feel so strongly about it that they try to stop even discussion or research on the genetics of race.

Q: You use twin studies to show how much is caused by genes and how much is caused by environment. Isn't it really the interaction of the two that matters?

A: Of course, every trait is the result of the interaction of heredity and environment. But if interaction is so important, why do identical twins who are brought up in different homes grow to be so much alike? It is because heredity plays a big role in development. The older we get, the more our genes, rather than our childhood environments, take control.

Q: Even if heredity is important for individuals, does that really tell us anything about race differences?

A: The evidence in Chapter 5 shows that genes do contribute a lot to race differences. Evidence comes from trans-racial adoption studies. Oriental, Mixed-Race (Black-White), and Black children adopted into middle-class White homes grow to resemble their true biological parents, not the White families who raised them. Mixed-Race (Black-White) infants grow up to have IQs between the IQs of pure Black and pure White children. Oriental children raised in White homes obtain IQs higher than White children, even if they were malnourished in infancy.

Q: But don't most experts believe that the cause of race differences in IQ is environmental, not genetic?

A: A survey done by Mark Snyderman and Stanley Rothman in the 1987 *American Psychologist* found that a majority (52%) of scientists said the Black-White IQ difference was partly genetic. Only 17% said it was entirely cultural. More recently, a special task force of the American Psychological Association agreed that there was a three-way pattern of race differences in brain size and IQ. Perhaps because of political correctness, the Task Force threw up its hands about the causes and decided to play it safe by saying "no one knows why" (see the 1996 and 1997 issues of the *American Psychologist*.)

Is *r-K* Theory Correct? (Chapter 6)

Q: You use *r-K* Life History Theory to explain race differences. You claim that Blacks are less *K* than Whites who are less *K* than Orientals. Haven't you twisted *r-K* theory to fit your own ideas about race differences?

A: Not at all. The key for understanding *K*-selection is the predictability of the environment. Tropical areas like Africa are less predictable because of parasites and sudden droughts. Therefore they select for an *r*-strategy rather than a *K*-strategy.

Q: Doesn't the *r-K* theory apply only to differences between different species, not to races within the same species?

A: It applies to both. Humans are very K compared to other species. Still, some people are more K than others. Highly K-selected men, for example, invest time and energy in their children rather than the pursuit of sexual thrills. They are "dads" rather than "cads." The r-K theory was first used to explain differences within species. I have applied it to race differences within humans.

Aren't Environmental Explanations Sufficient?
(Chapter 5)

Q: Couldn't the life-history differences you talk about just be the best response to *cultural* conditions? Since Blacks live in poor environments doesn't the r-strategy make sense? How can you invest if you have nothing to invest?

A: That could be, but the facts say no. Well-to-do college-educated Black women have more sexual intercourse at an earlier age and suffer greater infant mortality than do poorer White women who haven't gone to college. That fits with the r-K theory of race differences, but not with an environmental r-K theory. Orientals who have a poorer environment than Whites, have less sexual intercourse, start at a later age, and have lower infant mortality. Again, that fits with the r-K theory of race differences, but not with an environmental r-K theory.

Is Race Science Immoral? (Chapter 1)

Q: Why haven't I read this information on race differences in newspapers or seen it on TV? Isn't studying race differences immoral?

A: In the 1950s the liberation movements in the Third World and the Civil Rights Movement in the U.S. convinced many people, including journalists and politicians, that it was wrong to look at race differences. The goal of equal rights seemed to require not just political, but biological sameness. Many people wanted to believe that race differences were not at all genetic, and some were willing to distort the social sciences by separating them from the biological sciences. This book tries to put all the behavioral sciences back together again.

Q: Can any good come from your theory of race differences, even if it is true? Weren't theories about race differences the reason for racism, genocide and the Holocaust?

A: The Nazis and others used their supposed racial superiority to justify war and genocide. But just about every idea -- nationalism, religion, egalitarianism, even self-defence -- has been used as an excuse for war, oppression or genocide. Science, however, is objective. It can't give us our goals, but it can tell us how easy or difficult it will be to reach our goals. Knowing more about race differences may help us to give every child the best possible education and help us to understand some of our chronic social problems better.

Q: Wouldn't we be better off to ignore race and just treat each person as an individual?

A: Treating others as we would like to be treated is one of our highest ethical rules. So is telling the truth. The fact is that each of us is influenced by our genes and our environment. Treating people as individuals does not mean we should ignore or lie about race differences. Scientists have a special duty to examine the facts and report the truth.

Q: Why did the Charles Darwin Research Institute publish this Y2K version of the abridged edition? What happened to the original publisher?

A: Transaction Publishers printed 100,000 copies under their copyright. They sent 35,000 to scholars around the world — members of the American Anthropological Association, the American Psychological Association, the American Sociological Association, and the American Society for Criminology. Then the Progressive Sociologists, a self-proclaimed radical group within the American Sociological Association, along with some other "anti-racist" groups, threatened Transaction with loss of a booth at its annual meetings, advertising space in journals, and access to mailing lists if they continued to send out the abridged edition. Transaction caved in to this pressure, withdrew from publishing the abridged edition, and even apologized. They claimed that the Transaction copyright should never have appeared on the book and that it had "all been a mistake."

These events sadly confirm what I wrote in the first abridged edition -- that some vocal groups in academia and the media forbid an open discussion of race. They fear any open discussion of race research, all of which has appeared in peer-reviewed scientific journals. Truth, however, always wins out in the long run.

Closing Thoughts

The information in this book shows that the races differ in important ways. They differ, on average, in brain size, intelligence, sexual behavior, fertility, personality, maturation, life span, crime and in family stability. Orientals fall at one end of the three-way pattern of differences, Blacks fall at the other end, and Whites usually fall in between. Only a theory that looks at both genes and environment in terms of Darwin's theory of evolution can explain why the races differ so consistently throughout the world and over the course of time.

Both science and justice call for us to seek and tell the truth, not to tell lies and spread error. While the research in this book first appeared in peer-reviewed academic journals, many in the media, the government, and unfortunately even in the universities and colleges, skillfully avoid all such evidence. Hopefully this abridged edition will help set the record straight and make the latest scientific findings on race, evolution, and behavior open to all.

If we want to understand human behavior, the social sciences must get back together with the biological sciences. This book is a step in that direction. When we look at both genes and environment we may be able to understand human problems. With that knowledge, society can then go about trying to solve them. The first step is for all of us to be as honest as we can be about race, evolution, and behavior.

Additional Readings

Levin, M. (1997). *Why Race Matters*. New York: Praeger.

Rushton, J. P. (2000). *Race, Evolution, and Behavior (3rd ed.)*. New Brunswick, NJ: Transaction.

Index

Third Unabridged Edition of
Race, Evolution, and Behavior

This 400-page new *(Y2000)* edition contains over 1,000 references to the scholarly literature, a glossary, complete name and subject indexes, and 65 charts, maps, tables, and figures. It is an essential reference book for professionals and students of anthropology, psychology, sociology, and race relations. The **hardcover** unabridged *Race, Evolution, and Behavior* ($24) is especially appropriate for donation to public libraries, colleges and universities. The **softcover** unabridged edition ($14) provides a more economical way to order as a college or graduate school text.

Bulk Rate Ordering for
2nd Special Abridged Edition of
Race, Evolution, and Behavior

If you enjoyed reading this 110-page special abridged pocketbook, which summarizes important social and behavioral science research on race and race differences, you can order additional copies. Bulk rates are available for seminars, workshops, or for distribution to media figures (especially columnists who write about race issues), professors, teachers, and anyone interested in this vital subject.

Single copy $5.95
Bulk Rates

10 copies	$25.00	100 copies	$100.00
25 copies	$50.00	500 copies	$300.00
50 copies	$75.00	1000 copies	$400.00

All prices include postage & handling.

CHARLES DARWIN RESEARCH INSTITUTE
P.O. Box 611305, Port Huron, MI 48061-1305

Please send me ____copies of the abridged pocketbook edition of *Race, Evolution, and Behavior*. Enclosed is my check or money order for $_____ .

Name_____

Address_____

City/State/Zip_____

Country (if not USA)_____

Third Unabridged Edition of
Race, Evolution, and Behavior

This 400-page new *(Y2000)* edition contains over 1,000 references to the scholarly literature, a glossary, complete name and subject indexes, and 65 charts, maps, tables, and figures. It is an essential reference book for professionals and students of anthropology, psychology, sociology, and race relations. The **hardcover** unabridged *Race, Evolution, and Behavior* ($24) is especially appropriate for donation to public libraries, colleges and universities. The **softcover** unabridged edition ($14) provides a more economical way to order as a college or graduate school text.

CHARLES DARWIN RESEARCH INSTITUTE
P.O. Box 611305, Port Huron, MI 48061-1305
Please send me _____ copies of the **hardcover** ($24) unabridged edition of *Race, Evolution, and Behavior*. Or,_____copies of the **softcover** ($14) unabridged edition. Enclosed is my check or money order for $____ Add $4.50 postage and handling for 1st copy; $1.00 more for each additional book.

Name_____

Address_____

City/State/Zip_____

Country_____